KETO BREAD

Low-Carb Bakers Cookbook with Delicious Ketogenic Recipes for Boost Your Energy and Weight Loss

TABLE OF CONTENTS

INTRODUCTION

The Ketogenic diet plan has been recognized by many authorities on nutrition and weight loss. The diet plan is a scientifically proven weight loss program. Do you want to enjoy delicious and tasty bread and other baked goods while on the Ketogenic diet? Do you want low carb and gluten-free easy recipes for Ketogenic diet? Then this cookbook is for you. This cookbook will show you that you don't need to give up your bread choices. You can choose from healthy and delicious bread, biscuits, rolls, flatbread, breadsticks, muffins, crackers, and more.

This keto bread cookbook includes all the bread recipes that you thought you had to give up. These grain-free, low-carb read recipes are easy to make, and your whole family will love them. Every recipe in this book includes carb, protein, fat, and calories along with prep time, cook time, and servings to make your job easier. In this book, you will find out how you can still eat your keto bread and other baked goods that will satisfy your rumbling stomach but also make you feel good. Whether you are new to the keto diet or have been testing out the dishes for years, the recipes you will find here will help you prepare a healthy variety of bread that will make your mouth water.

CHAPTER 1 KETO BREAD

What is a Ketogenic Bread

For beginners, sticking to the Ketogenic diet is not easy. With the keto diet, you have to only consume low-carb, high-fat meals. To strictly follow the Keto diet, you need to eat only keto foods, including keto bread and bakery products. In this book, we will discuss how you can prepare your own keto bread and other healthy snacks in your free time at home. You may have some questions about the keto bread. How do they differ from the ordinary bread you purchase from the grocery store?

Unlike regular bread, keto bread is made without any flour, gluten, or sugar; it has almost no carbs. Keto bread is no different from the ordinary bread in terms of sponginess or texture when you take a bite. It is both tasty and can fully satisfy you in the same manner. However, the ingredients used make a big difference. Keto bread is simply a substitute for the ordinary bread.

The Main Keto bread ingredients

There are many types of keto bread for you to bake at home. As a result, there are many varying recipes of keto bread for you to pick from. Here are the main keto bread ingredients:

Butter

Butter has saturated fats, compared to carbohydrates and proteins, and a higher concentration of calories. It is a very versatile ingredient regardless of the recipe. It can be used in cooking, spreading, and baking. There are also different types of butter used in the keto diet. They are ghee, grass-fed butter, and clarified butter. Clarified butter is total fat without milk, lactose, or protein. It is good for an individual who is lactose intolerant. Ghee takes a bit longer to prepare compared to clarified butter. Grass-fed butter is the best since it contains higher levels of conjugated linoleic acid compared to commercial butter. Conjugated linoleic acid assists consumers in losing body fat.

Flour

You can use coconut flour, flax meal, ground flaxseed, almond meal, or almond flour when baking your keto bread. Remember, almond meal and almond flour are two different things. The almond meal is prepared from whole almonds, and the skin is removed to prepare the almond flour.

Coconut flour is another alternative to the wheat flour. The coconut flour is produced from coconut pulp after the raw product has been processed for its milk. Rich in fiber, healthy fats, and proteins, coconut flour is good for baking. However, because it has high fiber concentration, it is denser than regular flour. So you have to measure it exactly and work with a given ratio. When working on a given recipe requiring you to substitute wheat flour for coconut flour, the ratio will be 1:4. For a cup of regular wheat flour, you will substitute it with only a quarter cup of coconut flour.

Additionally, using eggs is important when using coconut flour. Eggs are a binding factor for the ingredients giving a good structure. Not using eggs will lead to poor cohesion and cause your meal to crumble. Use an egg for every quarter cup of coconut flour.

Macadamia nuts and flax seeds are two sources of keto flour. Flaxseeds are rich in dietary fiber and omega-3 fats. They are known as flax meal when consumed whole.

Sweeteners

Sweeteners can be used as a substitute for sugar. Remember, not all sweeteners are low-carb. For example, honey, a natural sweetener has more carb content than sugar. The keto sweeteners you can use for baking are monk fruit, erythritol, and stevia. They neither bring digestive complications nor increase your blood sugar levels. Obtained from plants, stevia, and monk fruit sweetener are natural sweeteners. Some people complain that stevia has a rather bitter aftertaste, but monk fruit sweetener has no aftertaste to it. Erythritol is a sugar alcohol produced from the fermentation of corn or birch. It has a cooling effect similar to mint, but you don't have to worry.

Baking powder

Use aluminum-free baking powder. Using aluminum-free baking powder ensures that you don't taste the baking powder when eating the bread.

Meet your macros with low-carb bread

You need to find out your daily macronutrient needs. You can use a keto calculator to know your macronutrient needs. Once you know how much you need to eat, you can start to figure out how to fit low carb bread into your diet. Here are some tips for meeting your fat needs when you are on a keto diet:

1. Add high-fat dairy like mascarpone cheese, cream cheese, and butter on top of your keto bread.

2. Eat some high-fat meat like bacon and pepperoni with less tasty or savory keto bread.

3. Add high-fat nuts like cashews and macadamias to bread like zucchini bread or pumpkin bread.

4. Spread mashed up avocado mixture (mixed with salt, pepper, and garlic powder) on top of your keto bread.

5. Eat your keto bread with your keto-friendly dressings, sauces, and dips.

Add more protein and fat to your bread

- Melt higher protein cheeses like parmesan, cheddar, and mozzarella on top of less tasty or savory keto bread.

- Make a sandwich with your favorite low-carb vegetables, cheese, and meats.

- Spread some natural almond butter or natural peanut butter on top of your favorite keto bread.

- Add crushed up high-protein nuts like almonds and pistachios on top of keto bread.

- Turn the keto zucchini bread or pumpkin bread into keto French toast.

CHAPTER 2. TIPS FOR KETO BAKING

Tips to help keto bread rise

- Use fresh baking powder. You can use the water test to know if your baking powder is fresh. Add a bit of baking powder in a glass of hot water. If it fizzes, it is fresh.
- Beat your eggs to get air into them and make them frothy. Avoid overbeating when adding your almond flour.
- Use room temperature eggs. If you use cooler eggs, then the dough will take more time to heat up, and it will lower the effectiveness of the baking powder.
- Don't use cold water. Use warm water.

Low-carb sandwich bread alternatives

- Zucchini: You can convert zucchinis into a keto open-faced sandwich. Scoop out most of the contents of the zucchini and fill it with keto savory ingredients. Make two of them and turn into a sub sandwich.
- Cucumber: Use the same method as zucchini.
- Eggplant: You can cut bigger eggplants crosswise, grill or bake them, and make an open-faced sandwich.

Useful tips for keto baking

1. Always sift your flour before start making your bread.
2. Avoid glass pans because they are poor conductors of heat. This causes your bread to be cooked before time.
3. If you don't have baking powder, you can use the combination of baking soda, lemon juice, and citric acid. Use 2 Tbsp. lemon juice with a single tsp. of baking soda.
4. Choose ingredients which are more natural and close to the source.
5. Add a pinch salt to counter the aftertaste of some sweeteners such as stevia. Some mix stevia and erythritol for better result.
6. The oven temperature and time to heat up may vary depending on oven model. Some models are more efficient than others. So don't solely depend on the recipe's stated cooking time.

7. Use butter or coconut oil to grease your baking pan. Also, double-grease by creating two layers on it.

8. Let your bread cool before slicing. The bread will get firmer when it is cooler.

Here are some more tips

- Read the instructions: Read the recipe instructions and follow them carefully.
- Lay it all out: Gather all the ingredients on your work station before starting baking bread.
- Buy a digital scale: A few ounces or few grams can make a big difference. You need to measure everything precisely. So buy a digital scale.
- Keep your eye on the oven: Don't leave your bread in the oven and forgot about it.
- Write in your bread diary: Write your experiences in your bread diary.
- Master a basic recipe, then experiment: You need to master basic bread recipes then move onto more complex ones.

CHAPTER 3.
BREAD RECIPES

Keto Breakfast Bread

Prep time: 15 minutes
Cook time: 40 minutes
Servings: 16 slices

Ingredients:

- ½ tsp. xanthan gum
- ½ tsp. salt
- 2 Tbsp. coconut oil
- ½ cup butter, melted
- 1 tsp. baking powder
- 2 cups of almond flour
- 7 eggs

Nutritional Facts Per Serving:

- Calories: 234
- Fat: 23g
- Carb: 1g
- Protein: 7g

Method:

1. Preheat the oven to 355F.
2. Beat eggs in a bowl on high for 2 minutes.
3. Add coconut oil and butter to the eggs and continue to beat.
4. Line a loaf pan with baking paper and pour the beaten eggs.
5. Pour in the rest of the ingredients and mix until it becomes thick.
6. Bake until a toothpick comes out dry, about 40 to 45 minutes.

Chia Seed Bread

Prep time: 10 minutes
Cook time: 40 minutes
Servings: 16 slices

Ingredients

- ½ tsp. xanthan gum
- ½ cup butter
- 2 Tbsp. coconut oil
- 1 Tbsp. baking powder
- 3 Tbsp. sesame seeds
- 2 Tbsp. chia seeds
- ½ tsp. salt
- ¼ cup sunflower seeds
- 2 cups almond flour
- 7 eggs

Nutritional Facts Per Serving:

- Calories: 405
- Fat: 37g
- Carb: 4g
- Protein: 14g

Method:

1. Preheat the oven to 350F.
2. Beat eggs in a bowl on high for 1 to 2 minutes.
3. Beat in the xanthan gum and combine coconut oil and melted butter into eggs, beating continuously.
4. Set aside the sesame seeds, but add the rest of the ingredients.
5. Line a loaf pan with baking paper and place the mixture in it. Top the mixture with sesame seeds.
6. Bake in the oven until a toothpick inserted comes out clean, about 35 to 40 minutes.

Keto Flax Bread

Prep time: 10 minutes
Cook time: 18 to 20 minutes
Servings: 8

Ingredients:

- ¾ cup of water
- 200 g ground flax seeds
- ½ cup psyllium husk powder
- 1 Tbsp. baking powder
- 7 large egg whites
- 3 Tbsp. butter
- 2 tsp. salt
- ¼ cup granulated stevia
- 1 large whole egg
- 1 ½ cups whey protein isolate

Nutritional Facts Per Serving:

- Calories: 265.5
- Fat: 15.68g
- Carb: 1.88g
- Protein:24.34 g

Method:

1. Preheat the oven to 350F.
2. Combine together whey protein isolate, psyllium husk, baking powder, sweetener, and salt.
3. In another bowl, mix together the water, butter, egg, and egg whites.
4. Slowly add psyllium husk mixture to egg mixture and mix well.
5. Lightly grease a bread pan with butter and pour in the batter.
6. Bake in the oven until the bread is set, about 18 to 20 minutes.

Special Keto Bread

Prep time: 15 minutes
Cook time: 40 minutes
Servings: 14

Ingredients:

- 2 tsp. baking powder
- ½ cup water
- 1 Tbsp. poppy seeds
- 2 cups fine ground almond meal
- 5 large eggs
- ½ cup olive oil
- ½ tsp. fine Himalayan salt

Nutritional Facts Per Serving:

- Calories: 227
- Fat: 21g
- Carb: 4g
- Protein: 7g

Method:

1. Preheat the oven to 400F.
2. In a bowl, combine salt, almond meal, and baking powder.
3. Drip in oil while mixing, until it forms a crumbly dough.
4. Make a little round hole in the middle of the dough and pour eggs into the middle of the dough.
5. Pour water and whisk eggs together with the mixer in the small circle until it is frothy.
6. Start making larger circles to combine the almond meal mixture with the dough until you have a smooth and thick batter.
7. Line your loaf pan with parchment paper.
8. Pour batter into the prepared loaf pan and sprinkle poppy seeds on top.
9. Bake in the oven for 40 minutes in the center rack until firm and golden brown.
10. Cool in the oven for 30 minutes.
11. Slice and serve.

Keto Easy Bread

Prep time: 15 minutes
Cook time: 45 minutes
Servings: 10

Ingredients:

- ¼ tsp. cream of tartar
- 1 ½ tsp. baking powder (double acting)
- 4 large eggs
- 1 ½ cups vanilla whey protein
- ¼ cup olive oil
- ¼ cup coconut milk, unsweetened
- ½ tsp. salt
- ¼ cup unsalted butter, softened
- 12 oz. cream cheese, softened
- ½ tsp. xanthan gum
- ½ tsp. baking soda

Nutritional Facts Per Serving:

- Calories: 294.2
- Fat: 24g
- Carb: 1.8g
- Protein: 17g

Method:

1. Preheat oven to 325F.
2. Layer aluminum foil over the loaf pan and spray with olive oil.
3. Beat the butter with cream cheese in a bowl until mixed well.
4. Add oil and coconut milk and blend until mixed. Add eggs, one by one until fully mixed. Set aside.
5. In a bowl, whisk whey protein, ½ tsp. xanthan gum, baking soda, cream of tartar, salt, and baking powder.
6. Add mixture to egg/cheese mixture and slowly mix until fully combined. Don't over blend.
7. Place in the oven and bake for 40 to 45 minutes, or until golden brown.
8. Cool, slice, and serve.

Almond Flour Apple Bread Rolls

Prep time: 10 minutes
Cook time: 30 minutes
Servings: 6

Ingredients:

- 1 cup boiling water or as needed
- 2 cups almond flour
- ½ cup ground flaxseed
- 4 Tbsp. psyllium husk powder
- 1 Tbsp. baking powder
- 2 Tbsp. olive oil
- 2 eggs
- 1 Tbsp. apple cider vinegar
- ½ tsp. salt

Nutritional Facts Per Serving:

- Calories: 301
- Fat: 24.1g
- Carb: 5g
- Protein: 11g

Method:

1. Preheat the oven to 350F.
2. In a bowl, mix together the almond flour, baking powder, psyllium husk powder, flax-seed flour, and salt.
3. Add the olive oil and eggs and blend until mixture resembles breadcrumbs, then mix in the apple cider vinegar.
4. Slowly add boiling water and mix into the mixture. Let stand for half an hour to firm up.
5. Line parchment paper over the baking tray.
6. Using your hands, make a ball of the dough.
7. Transfer dough balls on a baking tray and bake for 30 minutes, or until firm and golden.

Low Carb Bread

Prep time: 10 minutes
Cook time: 21 minutes
Servings: 12

Ingredients:

- 2 cups mozzarella cheese, grated
- 8 oz. cream cheese
- herbs and spices to taste
- 1 Tbsp. baking powder
- 1 cup crushed pork rinds
- ¼ cup parmesan cheese, grated
- 3 large eggs

Nutritional Facts Per Serving:

- Calories: 166
- Fat: 13g
- Carb: 1g
- Protein: 9g

Method:

1. Preheat oven to 375F.
2. Line parchment paper over the baking pan.
3. In a bowl, place cream cheese and mozzarella and microwave for 1 minute on high power. Stir and microwave for 1 minute more. Then stir again.
4. Stir in egg, parmesan, pork rinds, herbs, spices and baking powder until mixed.
5. Spread mixture on the baking pan and bake until top is lightly brown, about 15 to 20 minutes.
6. Cool, slice, and serve.

Splendid Low-Carb Bread

Prep time: 15 minutes
Cook time: 60 to 70 minutes
Servings: 12

Ingredients:

- ½ tsp. herbs, such as basil, rosemary, or oregano
- ½ tsp. garlic or onion powder
- 1 Tbsp. baking powder
- 5 Tbsp. psyllium husk powder
- ½ cup almond flour
- ½ cup coconut flour
- ¼ tsp. salt
- 1 ½ cup egg whites
- 3 Tbsp. oil or melted butter
- 2 Tbsp. apple cider vinegar
- 1/3 to ¾ cup hot water

Nutritional Facts Per Serving:

- Calories: 97
- Fat: 5.7g
- Carb: 7.5g
- Protein: 4.1g

Method:

1. Grease a loaf pan and preheat the oven to 350F.
2. In a bowl, whisk the salt, psyllium husk powder, onion or garlic powder, coconut flour, almond flour, and baking powder.
3. Stir in egg whites, oil, and apple cider vinegar. Bit by bit add the hot water, stirring until dough increase in size. Do not add too much water.
4. Mold the dough into a rectangle and transfer to grease loaf pan.
5. Bake in the oven for 60 to 70 minutes, or until crust feels firm and brown on top.
6. Cool and serve.

Bread De Soul

Prep time: 10 minutes
Cook time: 45 minutes
Servings: 16

Ingredients:

- ¼ tsp. cream of tartar
- 2 ½ tsp. baking powder
- 1 tsp. xanthan gum
- 1/3 tsp. baking soda
- ½ tsp. salt
- 1 2/3 cup unflavored whey protein
- ¼ cup olive oil
- ¼ cup heavy whipping cream or half and half
- 2 drops of sweet leaf stevia
- 4 eggs
- ¼ cup butter
- 12 oz. softened cream cheese

Nutritional Facts Per Serving:

- Calories: 200
- Fat: 15.2g
- Carb: 1.8g
- Protein: 10g

Method:

1. Preheat the oven to 325F.
2. In a bowl, microwave cream cheese and butter for 1 minute.
3. Remove and blend well with a hand mixer.
4. Add olive oil, eggs, heavy cream, and few drops of sweetener and blend well.
5. Blend together the dry ingredients in a separate bowl.
6. Combine the dry ingredients with the wet ingredients and mix with a spoon. Don't use a hand blender to avoid whipping it too much.
7. Grease a bread pan and pour the mixture into the pan.
8. Bake in the oven until golden brown, about 45 minutes.
9. Cool and serve.

Sandwich Flatbread

Prep time: 15 minutes
Cook time: 20 minutes
Servings: 10

Ingredients:

- ¼ cup water
- ¼ cup oil
- 4 eggs
- ½ tsp. salt
- 1/3 cup unflavored whey protein powder
- ½ tsp. garlic powder
- 2 tsp. baking powder
- 6 Tbsp. coconut flour
- 3 ¼ cups almond flour

Nutritional Facts Per Serving:

- Calories: 316
- Fat: 6.8g
- Carb: 11g
- Protein: 25.9g

Method:

1. Preheat the oven to 325F.
2. Combine the dry ingredients in a large bowl and mix with a hand whisk.
3. Whisk in eggs, oil, and water until combined well.
4. Place on a piece of large parchment paper and flatten into a rough rectangle. Place another parchment paper on top.
5. Roll into a large ½ inch to ¾ inch thick rough rectangle. Transfer to the baking sheet and discard the parchment paper on top.
6. Bake until it is firm to the touch, about 20 minutes.
7. Cool and cut into 10 portions.
8. Carefully cut each part into two halves through the bready center. Stuff with your sandwich fillings.
9. Serve.

Keto Sandwich Bread

Prep time: 5 minutes
Cook time: 1 hour
Servings: 12

Ingredients:

- 1 tsp. apple cider vinegar
- ¾ cup water
- ¼ cup avocado oil
- 5 eggs
- ½ tsp. salt
- 1 tsp. baking soda
- ½ cup coconut flour
- 2 cups plus 2 Tbsp. almond flour

Nutritional Facts Per Serving:

- Calories: 200g
- Fat: 7g
- Carb: 7g
- Protein: 16g

Method:

1. Preheat the oven to 350F and grease a loaf pan.
2. In a bowl, whisk almond flour, coconut flour, and salt.
3. In another bowl, separate the egg whites from egg yolks. Set egg whites aside.
4. In a blender, blend the oil, egg yolks, water, vinegar, and baking soda for 5 minutes on medium speed until combined.
5. Let the mixture sit for 1 minute then add in the reserved egg whites and mix until frothy, about 10 to 15 seconds.
6. Add the dry ingredients and process on high for 5 to 10 seconds before batter becomes too thick for the blender. Blend until the batter is smooth.
7. Transfer batter into the greased loaf pan and smoothen the top.
8. Bake in the oven until a skewer inserted comes out clean, about 50 to 70 minutes.
9. Cool, slice, and serve.

Coconut Flour Almond Bread

Prep time: 10 minutes
Cook time: 30 minutes
Servings: 4

Ingredients:

- 1 Tbsp. butter, melted
- 1 Tbsp. coconut oil, melted
- 6 eggs
- 1 tsp. baking soda
- 2 Tbsp. ground flaxseed
- 1 ½ Tbsp. psyllium husk powder
- 5 Tbsp. coconut flour
- 1 ½ cup almond flour

Nutritional Facts Per Serving:

- Calories: 475
- Fat: 38g
- Carb: 7g
- Protein: 19g

Method:

1. Preheat the oven to 400F.
2. Mix the eggs in a bowl for a few minutes.
3. Add in the butter and coconut oil and mix once more for 1 minute.
4. Add the almond flour, coconut flour, baking soda, psyllium husk, and ground flaxseed to the mixture. Let sit for 15 minutes.
5. Lightly grease the loaf pan with coconut oil. Pour the mixture in the pan.
6. Place in the oven and bake until a toothpick inserted in it comes out dry, about 25 minutes.

Easy Bake Keto Bread

Prep time: 10 minutes
Cook time: 30 minutes
Servings: 16

Ingredients:

- 7 whole eggs
- 4.5 oz. melted butter
- 2 Tbsp. warm water
- 2 tsp dry yeast
- 1 tsp. inulin
- 1 pinch of salt
- 1 tsp. xanthan gum
- 1 tsp. baking powder
- 1 Tbsp. psyllium husk powder
- 2 cups almond flour

Nutritional Facts Per Serving:

- Calories: 140
- Fat: 13g
- Carb: 3g
- Protein: 3g

Method:

1. Preheat the oven to 340F.
2. In a bowl, mix almond flour, salt, psyllium, baking powder, and xanthan gum.
3. Make a well in the center of the mixture.
4. Add the yeast and inulin into the center with the warm water.
5. Stir the inulin and yeast with the warm water in the center and let the yeast activate, about 10 minutes.
6. Add in the eggs and melted butter and stir well.
7. Pour the mixture into a loaf pan lined with parchment paper.
8. Allow batter to proof in a warm spot covered for 20 minutes with a tea towel.
9. Place in the oven and bake until golden brown, about 30 to 40 minutes.
10. Cool, slice, and serve.

Keto Bakers Bread

Prep time: 10 minutes
Cook time: 20 minutes
Servings: 12

Ingredients:

- pinch of salt
- 4 Tbsp. light cream cheese, softened
- ½ tsp. cream of tartar
- 4 eggs, yolks, and whites separated

Nutritional Facts Per Serving:

- Calories: 41
- Fat: 3.2g
- Carb: 1g
- Protein: 2.4g

Method:

1. Heat 2 racks in the middle of the oven at 350F.
2. Line 2 baking pan with parchment paper, then grease with cooking spray.
3. Separate egg yolks from the whites and place in separate mixing bowls.
4. Beat the egg whites and cream of tartar with a hand mixer until stiff, about 3 to 5 minutes. Do not over-beat.
5. Whisk the cream cheese, salt, and egg yolks until smooth.
6. Slowly fold the cheese mix into the whites until fluffy.
7. Spoon ¼ cup measure of the batter onto the baking sheets, 6 mounds on each sheet.
8. Bake in the oven for 20 to 22 minutes, alternating racks halfway through.
9. Cool and serve.

Keto Cloud Bread Cheese

Prep time: 5 minutes
Cook time: 30 minutes
Servings: 12

Ingredients for cream cheese filling:

- 1 egg yolk
- ½ tsp. vanilla stevia drops for filling
- 8 oz. softened cream cheese

Base egg dough:

- ½ tsp. cream of tartar
- 1 Tbsp. coconut flour
- ¼ cup unflavored whey protein
- 3 oz. softened cream cheese
- ¼ tsp. vanilla stevia drops for dough
- 4 eggs, separated

Nutritional Facts Per Serving:

- Calories: 120
- Fat: 10.7g
- Carb: 1.1g
- Protein: 5.4g

Method:

1. Preheat the oven to 325F.
2. Line two baking sheets with parchment paper.
3. In a bowl, stir the 8 ounces cream cheese, stevia, and egg yolk.
4. Transfer to the pastry bag.
5. In another bowl, separate egg yolks from whites.
6. Add 3 oz. cream cheese, yolks, stevia, whey protein, and coconut flour. Mix until smooth.
7. Whip cream of tartar with the egg whites until stiff peaks form.
8. Fold in the yolk/cream cheese mixture into the beaten whites.
9. Spoon batter onto each baking sheet, 6 mounds on each. Press each mound to flatten a bit.
10. Add cream cheese filling in the middle of each batter.
11. Bake for 30 minutes at 325F.

My Keto Bread

Prep time: 10 minutes

Cook time: 50 to 60 minutes

Servings: 6

Ingredients:

- 3 egg whites
- 1 cup of boiling water
- 2 Tbsp. sesame seeds
- 2 tsp. cider vinegar
- 1 tsp. sea salt
- 2 tsp. baking powder
- 5 Tbsp. ground psyllium husk powder
- 1 ¼ cups almond flour

Nutritional Facts Per Serving:

- Calories: 170
- Fat: 13g
- Carb: 2g
- Protein: 7g

Method:

1. Preheat the oven to 350F.
2. Mix the dry ingredients in a bowl.
3. In another bowl, add the boiling water, vinegar, and egg whites. Beat for 30 seconds with a hand mixer. Don't over mix.
4. Grease hands with oil to make 6 pieces then arrange on a greased baking sheet.
5. Bake 50 to 60 minutes in the lower rack of the oven. Cooking time depends on the size of the bread. The bread is ready when it makes a hollow sound when tapped.

Keto Oat Cornbread

Prep time: 10 minutes
Cook time: 20 minutes
Servings: 8

Ingredients:

- ¼ tsp. corn extract
- 4 eggs
- ¼ cup water
- 1/3 cup melted bacon fat or coconut oil
- 4 oz. melted butter
- ¼ tsp. salt
- 1 ½ tsp. baking powder
- 1/3 cup whey protein isolate, unflavored
- ½ cup oat fiber
- ¼ cup coconut flour

Nutritional Facts Per Serving:

- Calories: 240
- Fat: 23g
- Carb: 1g
- Protein: 7g

Method:

1. Preheat oven to 350F.
2. Grease a 10-inch cast iron skillet and place in the oven to warm up.
3. Combine all the dry ingredients in a bowl. Add the eggs, water, melted butter, and bacon fat. Beat with a hand mixer, then mix in corn extract.
4. Transfer mixture into the heated skillet.
5. Bake at 350F for 18 to 20 minutes or until firm and top is lightly browned.

Almond Flour Lemon Bread

Prep time: 15 minutes
Cook time: 45 minutes
Servings: 16

Ingredients:

- 1 tsp. French herbs
- 1 tsp. lemon juice
- 1 tsp. salt
- 1 tsp. cream of tartar
- 2 tsp. baking powder
- ¼ cup melted butter
- 5 large eggs, divided
- ¼ cup coconut flour
- 1 ½ cup almond flour

Nutritional Facts Per Serving:

- Calories: 115
- Fat: 9.9g
- Carb: 3.3g
- Protein: 5.2g

Method:

1. Preheat the oven to 350F.
2. Whip the whites and cream of tartar until soft peaks form.
3. In a bowl, combine salt, egg yolks, melted butter, and lemon juice. Mix well.
4. Add coconut flour, almond flour, herbs, and baking powder. Mix well.
5. To the dough, add 1/3 the egg whites and mix until well-combined.
6. Add the remaining egg whites mixture and slowly mix to incorporate everything. Do not over mix.
7. Grease a loaf pan with butter or coconut oil.
8. Pour mixture into the loaf pan and bake for 30 minutes.

Cheesy Keto Sesame Bread

Prep time: 5 minutes
Cook time: 30 minutes
Servings: 8

Ingredients:

- 1 tsp. sesame seeds
- 1 tsp. baking powder
- 1 tsp. salt
- 2 Tbsp. ground psyllium husk powder
- 1 cup almond flour
- 4 Tbsp. sesame or olive oil
- 7 ounces cream cheese
- 4 eggs
- Sea salt

Nutritional Facts Per Serving:

- Calories: 282
- Fat: 26g
- Carb: 2g
- Protein: 7g

Method:

1. Preheat the oven to 400F.
2. Beat the eggs until fluffy. Add cream cheese and oil until combined well.
3. Set the sesame seeds aside and add the remaining ingredients.
4. Grease a baking tray. Spread the dough in the greased baking tray. Allow it to stand for 5 minutes.
5. Baste dough with oil and top with a sprinkle of sesame seeds and a little sea salt.
6. Bake in the oven at 400F until the top is golden brown, about 30 minutes.

Blueberry Bread Loaf

Prep time: 20 minutes
Cook time: 65 minutes
Servings: 12

Ingredients for the bread dough:

- 10 Tbsp. coconut flour
- 9 Tbsp. melted butter
- 2/3 cup granulates swerve sweetener
- 1 ½ tsp. baking powder
- 2 Tbsp. heavy whipping cream
- 1 ½ tsp. vanilla extract
- ½ tsp. cinnamon
- 2 Tbsp. sour cream
- 6 large eggs
- ½ tsp. salt
- ¾ cup blueberries

For the topping:

- 1 Tbsp. heavy whipping cream
- 2 Tbsp. confectioner swerve sweetener
- 1 tsp. melted butter
- 1/8 tsp. vanilla extract
- ¼ tsp. lemon zest

Nutritional Facts Per Serving:

- Calories: 155
- Fat: 13g
- Carb: 4g
- Protein: 3g

Method:

1. Preheat the oven to 350F and line a loaf pan with baking paper.
2. In a bowl, mix granulated swerve, heavy whipping cream, eggs, and baking powder.
3. Once combined, add the butter, vanilla extract, salt, cinnamon, and sour cream. Then add the coconut flour to the batter.
4. Pour a layer about ½ inch of dough into the bread pan. Place ¼ cup blueberries on top of the dough. Keep repeating until the dough and blueberry layers are complete.
5. Bake for 65 to 75 minutes.
6. Meanwhile, in a bowl, beat the vanilla extract, butter, heavy whipping cream, lemon zest, and confectioner swerve. Mix until creamy.
7. Cool the bread once baked. Then drizzle the icing topping on the bread.
8. Slice and serve.

Cauliflower Bread Loaf

Prep time: 1 hour 10 minutes

Cook time: 45 minutes

Servings: 10

Ingredients for the bread dough:

- 1 ¼ cups of almond flour
- 3 cup of riced cauliflower
- 1 Tbsp. baking powder
- 6 Tbsp. of olive oil
- 6 large eggs, separated
- 1 tsp. salt

Optional flavorings:

- dried or fresh herbs
- shredded parmesan or cheddar cheese
- garlic powder or minced garlic

Nutritional Facts Per Serving:

- Calories: 155
- Fat: 13g
- Carb: 4g
- Protein: 3g

Method:

1. Preheat the oven to 350F. Line a bread loaf with baking paper.
2. Place cauliflower into the small pot to steam until it becomes tender. Place it to the side.
3. Cream the whites of the eggs in a food processor for 4 minutes. Set to the side.
4. In a bowl, whisk the egg yolks, and almond flour until mixed well. Next, add the baking powder, oil, and salt and mix until smooth.
5. Remove excess fluid from the cooled cauliflower with a paper towel.
6. Stir in the dried cauliflower and mix well. Add the flavoring ingredients.
7. In small amounts, fold the egg white mixture to the mixture until fluffy. Don't overbeat.
8. Transfer the dough into the bread loaf pan.
9. Bake in the oven for 45 minutes. Test with a knife.
10. Cool, slice, and serve.

Cheese and Bacon Bread Loaf

Prep time: 1 hour

Cook time: 45 to 50 minutes

Servings: 10

Ingredients:

- 1/3 cup sour cream
- 4 Tbsp. melted butter
- 1 ½ cups almond flour
- 1 cup grated cheese
- 1 Tbsp. baking powder
- 2 large eggs
- 7 ounces bacon

Nutritional Facts Per Serving:

- Calories: 292
- Fat: 13g
- Carb: 4g
- Protein: 3g

Method:

1. Preheat oven to 300F. Line the loaf pan with baking paper.
2. Cut and dice the bacon and cook until crispy.
3. In a bowl, mix almond flour and baking powder with a fork.
4. Using a hand mixer, cream the sour cream and eggs into the flour mix. Add to the mixed dry ingredients along with cooled butter and combine well.
5. Fold in the grated cheese and cooked bacon into the dough.
6. Empty the dough into the bread loaf pan. Sprinkle the top with extra cheese if you want the bread to be extra cheesy.
7. Bake in the oven for 45 to 50 minutes.
8. Cool, slice, and serve.

Hearty Seeded Bread Loaf

Prep time: 1 hour 10 minutes

Cook time: 1 hour

Servings: 16

Ingredients:

- 1 ½ cups pumpkin seeds (1 cup finely chopped with a food processor)
- ½ cup whole psyllium husks
- ½ cup flax seeds
- ½ cup chia seeds
- 1 ½ cups warm water
- 1 tsp. pink salt
- 1 cup raw sunflower seeds
- 1 Tbsp. maple syrup
- 3 Tbsp. melted coconut oil

Nutritional Facts Per Serving:

- Calories: 172
- Fat: 6g
- Carb: 2g
- Protein: 7g

Method:

1. Preheat the oven to 350F. Line a loaf pan with parchment paper.

2. In a bowl, pour in the ½ cup whole pumpkin seeds, pumpkin seed flour, sunflower seeds, psyllium husks, chia seed, flax seeds, and salt.

3. Pour the maple syrup, warm water, and melted coconut oil into a bowl and continue stirring until the batter becomes thick.

4. Pack the batter by hand into the lined bread loaf pan.

5. Bake the loaf for 45 minutes and remove from the pan.

6. On a sheet of baking paper, put the bread loaf, turn over on the top, and remove the bread pan from the loaf of bread.

7. Return the bread to the oven to continue cooking for 15 minutes more.

8. Cool, slice, and serve.

Quick Low-Carb Bread Loaf

Prep time: 45 minutes

Cook time: 40 to 45 minutes

Servings: 16

Ingredients:

- 2/3 cup coconut flour
- ½ cup butter, melted
- 3 Tbsp. coconut oil, melted
- 1 1/3 cup almond flour
- ½ tsp. xanthan gum
- 1 tsp. baking powder
- 6 large eggs
- ½ tsp. salt

Nutritional Facts Per Serving:

- Calories: 174
- Fat: 15g
- Carb: 5g
- Protein: 5g

Method:

1. Preheat the oven to 350F. Cover the bread loaf pan with baking paper.
2. Beat the eggs until creamy.
3. Add in the coconut flour and almond flour, mixing them for 1 minute. Next, add the xanthan gum, coconut oil, baking powder, butter, and salt and mix them until the dough turns thick.
4. Put the completed dough into the prepared line of the bread loaf pan.
5. Place in oven and bake for 40 to 45 minutes. Check with a knife.
6. Slice and serve.

Savory Bread Loaf

Prep time: 1 minutes

Cook time: 50 to 55 minutes

Servings: 12

Ingredients:

- ¼ cup coconut flour
- 8 eggs
- 8 ounces cream cheese
- 2 ½ cups almond flour
- ½ cup butter
- 1 tsp. rosemary
- 1 ½ tsp. baking powder
- 1 tsp. sage
- 2 Tbsp. parsley

Nutritional Facts Per Serving:

- Calories: 202
- Fat: 20g
- Carb: 5g
- Protein: 6g

Method:

1. Preheat the oven to 350F. Line a loaf pan with parchment paper.

2. In a bowl, combine the butter, rosemary, parsley, sage, and sour cream until fluffy and mixed well.

3. In the mixture, whisk each egg and repeat until all eggs are mixed into the mixture and are smooth.

4. Add the almond and coconut flour and the baking powder and combine them thoroughly resulting in a thick dough.

5. Pour the completed dough in the lined bread loaf pan.

6. Heat the bread loaf in the stove for 50 to 55 minutes. Check the middle to ensure it is baked properly.

CHAPTER 4. OTHER BAKED RECIPES

Breadsticks

Prep time: 5 minutes

Cook time: 15 minutes

Servings: 10

Ingredients:

- 2 eggs
- 1 ½ Tbsp. olive oil
- ½ tsp. oregano
- ½ tsp. parsley
- ½ tsp. basil
- ½ tsp. garlic powder
- ½ tsp. onion powder
- 2 ½ Tbsp. coconut flour
- 2 cups almond flour

Topping:

- ¼ tsp. salt
- ½ tsp. garlic powder
- 2 tsp. parmesan grated
- 1 Tbsp. olive oil

Nutritional Facts Per Serving:

- Calories: 169
- Fat: 15.15g
- Carb: 6.14g
- Protein: 6.65g

Method:

1. Preheat the oven to 350F and line a baking pan with parchment paper.
2. In a bowl, whisk almond flour, olive oil, and seasoning.
3. Whisk the eggs in another bowl, mix into the almond flour.
4. Add 1 tbsp. coconut flour to the mixture at a time, stirring to combine.
5. Allow dough to rest for 1 to 2 minutes after each tbsp. Once the mixture gets thick, add the remaining coconut flour.
6. Form dough into a ball, about 2 tbsp. and roll out into 1.5-inch wide rope-like sticks.
7. Transfer to the prepared baking sheet, place in the oven, and bake for 10 minutes.
8. Meanwhile, mix together salt, parmesan, and garlic.
9. Once baked, carefully brush the tops of breadsticks with oil, then sprinkle with garlic parmesan mix.
10. Bake for 5 minutes more.

Low-Carb Bagel

Prep time: 15 minutes
Cook time: 25 minutes
Servings: 12

Ingredients:

- 1 cup protein powder, unflavored
- 1/3 cup coconut flour
- 1 tsp. baking powder
- ½ tsp. sea salt
- ¼ cup ground flaxseed
- 1/3 cup sour cream
- 12 eggs

Seasoning topping:

- 1 tsp. dried parsley
- 1 tsp. dried oregano
- 1 tsp. dried minced onion
- ½ tsp. garlic powder
- ½ tsp. dried basil
- ½ tsp. sea salt

Nutritional Facts Per Serving:

- Calories: 134
- Fat: 6.8g
- Carb: 4.2g
- Protein: 12.1g

Method:

1. Preheat the oven to 350F.

2. In a mixer, blend sour cream and eggs until well combined.

3. Whisk together the flaxseed, salt, baking powder, protein powder, and coconut flour in a bowl.

4. Gently mix the dry ingredients into the wet ingredients until well blended.

5. Whisk the topping seasoning together in a small bowl. Set aside.

6. Grease 2 donut pans that can contain 6 donuts each.

7. Sprinkle pan with about 1 tsp. topping seasoning and evenly pour batter into each.

8. Sprinkle the top of each bagel evenly with the rest of the seasoning mixture.

9. Bake in the oven for 25 minutes, or until golden brown.

10. Cool and serve.

Cheddar Sausage Biscuits

Prep time: 15 minutes
Cook time: 25 minutes
Servings: 8

Ingredients:

- 6 oz. cooked sausage, grease drained, thinly sliced
- ¼ cup water
- ¼ cup heavy cream
- 1 cup shredded sharp white cheddar cheese
- 1 ½ cups almond flour
- ½ tsp. Italian seasoning
- ½ tsp. sea salt
- 1 Tbsp. chopped fresh chives
- 2 minced large garlic cloves
- 1 large egg
- 4 oz. softened cream cheese

Nutritional Facts Per Serving:

- Calories: 321
- Fat: 28g
- Carb: 3.5g
- Protein: 13g

Method:

1. Preheat the oven to 350F.
2. Using a hand mixer on low speed, whip the eggs and cream cheese in a bowl.
3. Add the garlic, chives, sea salt, Italian seasoning, then mix into the egg cheese mixture.
4. Add the water, almond flour, heavy cream, and cheddar cheese. Mix well.
5. Slowly mix in the sausage into the mixture using a spatula.
6. Lightly grease muffin pan.
7. Drop a heap mold of dough into 8 wells on the muffin top pan.
8. Bake in the oven for 25 minutes.
9. Cool and serve.

Low-Carb Pretzels

Prep time: 15 minutes
Cook time: 15 minutes
Servings: 12

Ingredients:

- 1 Tbsp. pretzel salt
- 2 Tbsp. butter, melted
- 2 Tbsp. warm water
- 2 tsp. dried yeast
- 2 eggs
- 2 tsp. xanthan gum
- 1 ½ cups almond flour
- 4 tbsp. cream cheese
- 3 cups of shredded mozzarella cheese

Nutritional Facts Per Serving:

- Calories: 217
- Fat: 18g
- Carb: 3g
- Protein: 11g

Method:

1. Preheat the oven to 390F.
2. Melt the mozzarella cheese and cream cheese in the microwave.
3. Combine warm water with yeast and let sit for 2 minutes and activate.
4. Mix the almond meal and xanthan gum with a hand mixer.
5. Add yeast mixture, 1 tbsp. melted butter, and eggs and mix well.
6. Add in the melted cheese and knead the dough, about 5 to 10 minutes or until well combined.
7. Divide into 12 balls while the dough is still warm, then roll into a long, thin log and then twist to form a pretzel shape.
8. Transfer onto a lined cookie sheet, leaving small space between them.
9. Brush the remaining butter on top the pretzels and sprinkle with the salt.
10. Bake for 12 to 15 minutes in the oven or until golden brown.

Shortbread Vanilla Cookies

Prep time: 15 minutes
Cook time: 20 minutes
Servings: 16

Ingredients:

- 1 egg
- ½ cup unsalted butter, softened
- 1 tsp. vanilla extract
- 1 pinch salt
- 1/3 cup erythritol
- 2 cups almond flour

Nutritional Facts Per Serving:

- Calories: 126
- Fat: 12g
- Carb: 2g
- Protein: 3g

Method:

1. Preheat the oven to 300F.
2. Mix together the almond flour, erythritol, salt, and vanilla extract in a bowl.
3. Pour in butter and mix with the almond flour mix unit well combined. Add egg and mix well.
4. Roll one Tbsp. mixture into a ball. Place them onto a lined cookie sheet with gaps in between. Press.
5. Place in the oven and bake for 12 to 25 minutes, or until the edges are browned.
6. Cool and serve.

Low-Carb Taco Shells

Prep time: 10 minutes
Cook time: 15 minutes
Servings: 4

Ingredients:

- ½ tsp. ground cumin
- 8 ounces shredded cheese

Nutritional Facts Per Serving:

- Calories: 202
- Fat: 16g
- Carb: 1g
- Protein: 13g

Method:

1. Preheat the oven to 400F.
2. Mix together the cumin and cheese.
3. Line a baking sheet with parchment paper.
4. Drop 6 to 8 heaps of the cheese on the prepared sheet with. Keep enough space between them.
5. Bake until cheese is bubbling with golden brown patches, about 10 to 15 minutes. Be careful not to burn the cheese.
6. Allow to cool for half a minute.
7. Place a rack on the sink and gently arrange cheese tortillas over the rack.
8. Before cheese cools down completely, let each round's edges drop down between the rack's bars to from taco shell shape.

Keto Buns

Prep time: 5 minutes
Cook time: 26 minutes
Servings: 6

Ingredients:

- 1 tsp. onion flakes
- 1 Tbsp. black sesame seeds
- 1 Tbsp. white sesame seeds
- 1 tsp. rosemary
- 3.5 oz. almond flour
- ½ tsp. Himalayan salt
- 4 eggs
- 4 Tbsp. unsalted butter

Nutritional Facts Per Serving:

- Calories: 230
- Fat: 20.82g
- Carb: 3.99g
- Protein: 8.45g

Method:

1. Preheat the oven to 430F.
2. Add the eggs and melted butter inside a stick blender beaker.
3. Add the remaining ingredients and place the stick blender into the beaker. Pulse until batter is fully mixed.
4. Take 6 silicone jumbo muffin molds and evenly pour the batter. If desired, sprinkle top of each bun with extra sesame seeds.
5. Bake in the oven at 430F for 26 minutes.
6. Cool, slice, and serve.

Goat Cheese Crackers

Prep time: 5 minutes
Cook time: 20 minutes
Servings: 12

Ingredients:

- 6 oz. goat cheese
- ½ cup coconut flour
- 4 Tbsp. butter
- 2 Tbsp. fresh rosemary
- 1 tsp. baking powder

Nutritional Facts Per Serving:

- Calories: 99
- Fat: 8g
- Carb: 2g
- Protein: 4g

Method:

1. In a food processor, combine all ingredients and mix until smooth.
2. Roll out the dough with a rolling pin to about ¼ to ½ inch thick and cut out the crackers with a knife or cookie cutter.
3. Line a baking sheet with parchment paper and place the crackers on it.
4. Bake at 380F for 15 to 20 minutes.

Chocolate chip Cookies

Prep time: 10 minutes
Cook time: 15 minutes
Servings: 15

Ingredients:

- 1 cup chocolate flour
- ½ cup butter, softened
- 1 cup unsweetened coconut flakes
- 4 eggs
- 2 2/3 oz. dark chocolate chips
- ½ tsp. vanilla extract
- ½ cup erythritol

Nutritional Facts Per Serving:

- Calories: 195
- Fat: 16g
- Carb: 5g
- Protein: 4g

Method:

1. Mix the erythritol, butter, vanilla, eggs, and salt together.
2. Add the chocolate chips, coconut flakes, and coconut flour. Mix well.
3. Line a baking sheet with parchment paper and spoon the cookies onto it.
4. Bake at 375F for 15 to 20 minutes.

Buns with Cottage Cheese

Prep time: 10 minutes
Cook time: 15 minutes
Servings: 8

Ingredients:

- 2 eggs
- 3 oz. almond flour
- 1 oz. erythritol
- 1/8 tsp. stevia
- cinnamon and vanilla extract to taste

Filling:

- 5 ½ oz. cottage cheese
- 1 egg
- Cinnamon and vanilla extract to taste

Nutritional Facts Per Serving:

- Calories: 77
- Fat: 5.2g
- Carb: 6.7g
- Protein: 5.8g

Method:

1. Prepare the filling by mixing its ingredients in a bowl.
2. Combine eggs with almond flour, blend until smooth. Add erythritol, stevia, and flavors to taste.
3. Spoon 1 Tbsp. dough into silicone cups. Spoon about 1 tsp. filling on top, and bake at 365F for 15 minutes.

Sandwich Buns

Prep time: 10 minutes
Cook time: 25 minutes
Servings: 8

Ingredients:

- 4 eggs
- 2 ½ oz. almond flour
- 1 Tbsp. coconut flour
- 1 oz. psyllium
- 1 ½ cups eggplant, finely grated, juices drained
- 3 Tbsp. sesame seeds
- 1 ½ tsp. baking powder
- Salt to taste

Nutritional Facts Per Serving:

- Calories: 99
- Fat: 6g
- Carb: 10g
- Protein: 5.3g

Method:

1. Whisk eggs until foamy, and then add grated eggplant.
2. In a separate bowl, mix all dry ingredients.
3. Add them to the egg mixture. Mix well.
4. Line a baking sheet with parchment paper and shape the buns with your hands.
5. Bake at 374F for 20 to 25 minutes.

Keto Pizza

Prep time: 10 minutes
Cook time: 20 minutes
Servings: 1

Ingredients:

- 2 eggs
- 2 Tbsp. parmesan cheese
- 1 Tbsp. psyllium husk powder
- ½ tsp. Italian seasoning
- salt
- 2 tsp. frying oil
- 1 ½ ounce mozzarella cheese
- 3 Tbsp. tomato sauce
- 1 Tbsp. chopped basil

Nutritional Facts Per Serving:

- Calories: 459
- Fat: 35g
- Carb: 3.5g
- Protein: 27g

Method:

1. In a blender, place the parmesan, psyllium husk powder, Italian seasoning, salt, and two eggs and blend.
2. Heat a large frying pan and add the oil.
3. Add the mixture to the pan in a large circular shape.
4. Flip once the underside is browning and then remove from the pan.
5. Spoon the tomato sauce onto the pizza crust and spread.
6. Add the cheese and spread over the top of the pizza.
7. Place the pizza into the oven – it is done once the cheese is melted.
8. Top the pizza with basil.

Pizza Frittata

Prep time: 15 minutes
Cook time: 30 minutes
Servings: 8

Ingredients:

- 12 eggs
- 9-ounce bag frozen spinach
- 1-ounce pepperoni
- 5 ounces mozzarella cheese
- 1 tsp. garlic, minced
- ½ cup ricotta cheese
- ½ cup parmesan cheese
- 4 Tbsp. olive oil
- ¼ tsp. nutmeg
- Salt and pepper to taste

Nutritional Facts Per Serving:

- Calories: 298
- Fat: 23.8g
- Carb: 2.1g
- Protein: 19.4g

Method:

1. Microwave the spinach on defrost.
2. Preheat the oven to 375F.
3. Combine the spinach, parmesan, ricotta and other ingredients besides mozzarella and pepperoni.
4. Pour the mixture into a baking dish.
5. Sprinkle the mozzarella over the mixture.
6. Add the pepperoni.
7. Bake for half an hour, until set.

Iranian Flatbread

Prep time: 3 hours 15 minutes

Cook time: 6 minutes

Servings: 6

Ingredients:

- 4 cups almond flour
- 2 ½ cups warm water
- 1 Tbsp. instant yeast
- 12 tsp. sesame seeds
- Salt to taste

Nutritional Facts Per Serving:

- Calories: 26
- Fat: 1g
- Carb: 3.5g
- Protein: 1g

Method:

1. In a bowl, add 1 Tbsp. yeast to ½ cup warm water. Let stand for 5 minutes to activate.

2. Add salt and 1 cup water. Let stand for 10 minutes more.

3. Add flour 1 cup at a time, and then add the remaining water.

4. Knead the dough and then shape into a ball and let stand for 3 hours covered.

5. Preheat the oven to 480F.

6. With a rolling pin, roll out the dough and divide into 6 balls. Roll each ball into ½ inch thick rounds.

7. Line a baking sheet with parchment paper and place the rolled rounds on it. With a finger, make a small hole in the middle and add 2 tsp. sesame seeds in each hole.

8. Bake for 3 to 4 minutes and then flip over and bake for 2 minutes more.

Fathead Rolls

Prep time: 10 minutes
Cook time: 12 minutes
Servings: 4

Ingredients:

- ¾ cup shredded mozzarella cheese
- 3 oz. cream cheese
- ½ cup shredded cheddar cheese
- 1 beaten egg
- ¼ tsp. garlic powder
- 1/3 cup almond flour
- 2 tsp. baking powder

Nutritional Facts Per Serving:

- Calories: 160
- Fat: 13g
- Carb: 2.5g
- Protein: 7g

Method:

1. Preheat the oven to 425F.
2. Combine the cream cheese and mozzarella. Place in the microwave and cook for 20 seconds at a time until cheese melts.
3. Beat the eggs in another bowl and add the dry ingredients.
4. Work in the mozzarella. Stir in cheddar cheese. Scoop the dough into a sheet of plastic wrap. Sprinkle the top of the bread with the almond flour.
5. Fold the plastic wrap over the dough. Gently start working into a ball. Cover and place in the fridge for ½ hour.
6. Slice the dough ball into four sections and roll each one into a ball. Cut the ball in half.
7. Place the cut side down onto a well-greased sheet pan.
8. Bake for 10 to 12 minutes.

Cream Cheese Rolls

Prep time: 10 minutes
Cook time: 40 minutes
Servings: 6

Ingredients:

- 3 eggs
- 3 oz. full-fat cream cheese, cubed and cold
- ¼ tsp. cream of tartar
- ¼ tsp. salt

Nutritional Facts Per Serving:

- Calories: 91.3
- Fat: 8g
- Carb: 1g
- Protein: 4.2g

Method:

1. Preheat the oven to 300F.
2. Line a baking pan with parchment paper. Grease with cooking oil
3. Separate the yolks from the eggs and place the whites in a container. Whisk with the tartar until stiff.
4. In another container, whisk the cream cheese, salt, and yolks until smooth.
5. Fold in the whites of the eggs, mixing well with a spatula. Mold a scoop of whites over the yolk mixture and fold together as you rotate the dish. Continue unit well combined.
6. Place six large spoons of the mixture onto the prepared pan. Mash the tops with the spatula to slightly flatten.
7. Bake until browned, about 30 to 40 minutes.
8. Cool a few minutes in the pan. Then, carefully arrange them on a wire rack to cool.

Onion Bagels

Prep time: 15 minutes
Cook time: 30 minutes
Servings: 6

Ingredients:

- 2 Tbsp. coconut flour
- 3 Tbsp. flaxseed meal
- ½ tsp. baking powder
- 4 eggs, separated
- 1 tsp. dried minced onion

Nutritional Facts Per Serving:

- Calories: 78
- Fat: 5g
- Carb: 1g
- Protein: 5g

Method:

1. Preheat the oven to 325F. Grease a donut pan with cooking spray.
2. Sift the flax meal, coconut flour, minced onion, and baking powder.
3. Whip the egg whites until foamy. Slowly whisk in the yolks and dry mixture. Let the dough thicken for 5 to 10 minutes.
4. Scoop into the molds and sprinkle with a portion of dried onion to your liking.
5. Bake for 30 minutes, or until golden brown.
6. Cool and serve.

Poppy and Sesame Seed Bagels

Prep time: 10 minutes
Cook time: 15 minutes
Servings: 6

Ingredients:

- 8 tsp. sesame seeds
- 8 tsp. poppy seeds
- 4 oz. cream cheese
- 2 ½ cups shredded mozzarella cheese
- 1 tsp. baking powder
- 1 ½ cups almond flour
- 2 eggs

Method:

1. Preheat the oven to 400F. Prepare a baking sheet with a layer of parchment paper. Combine the almond flour and baking powder.
2. Melt the cream cheese and mozzarella in the microwave.
3. Whisk the eggs and add the cheese mixture. Stir to combine with the rest of the fixings. Once the dough is formed, divide it into six pieces.
4. Stretch the dough and join the ends to form the bagel. Arrange on the baking sheet.
5. Sprinkle with the seed combination and bake for 15 minutes.

Nutritional Facts Per Serving:

- Calories: 350
- Fat: 29g
- Carb: 5g
- Protein: 20g

Pumpkin Muffins

Prep time: 10 minutes
Cook time: 18 minutes
Servings: 5

Ingredients:

- ½ tsp. salt
- ½ tsp. baking powder
- 1 egg
- 1 Tbsp. vanilla extract
- 1 Tbsp. apple cider vinegar
- ½ cup pumpkin puree
- 2 Tbsp. coconut oil
- ¼ cup sugar-free caramel syrup
- ¼ cup crushed almonds

Nutritional Facts Per Serving:

- Calories: 185
- Fat: 13.5g
- Carb: 3.5g
- Protein: 7.4g

Method:

1. Preheat the oven to 350F.
2. Combine all of the components in the recipe list except for the almonds.
3. Prepare a muffin pan for 5 portions and spritz with oil.
4. Cover with crushed almonds.
5. Bake for 15 to 18 minutes.

Squash Muffins

Prep time: 10 minutes
Cook time: 25 minutes
Servings: 6

Ingredients:

- salt to taste
- ½ tsp. baking powder
- 1 cup almond flour
- 1 peeled and grated squash
- 2 to 3 springs chopped spring onions
- 1 Tbsp. olive oil
- 1 egg
- ¼ cup plain yogurt
- ½ cup grated hard cheese

Nutritional Facts Per Serving:

- Calories: 111
- Fat: 7.8g
- Carb: 3.4g
- Protein: 7.3g

Method:

1. Preheat the oven to 350F. Spray muffin tins with cooking spray.
2. Season the grated squash with salt and set aside.
3. Combine the sifted flour, salt, and baking powder.
4. Whisk the egg, and mix with the oil, yogurt, and ½ of the cheese. Combine the fixings.
5. Add the squash and juices to the dough.
6. Work in the chopped onions and add to the prepared muffin cups.
7. Sprinkle with the cheese and bake for 25 minutes.
8. Cool and serve.

Garlic Breadsticks

Prep time: 10 minutes
Cook time: 20 minutes
Servings: 8

Ingredients for the garlic butter:

- ¼ cup butter, softened
- 1 tsp. garlic powder

Other ingredients:

- 2 cups almond flour
- ½ Tbsp. baking powder
- 1 Tbsp. psyllium husk powder
- ¼ tsp. salt
- 3 Tbsp. butter, melted
- 1 egg
- ¼ cup boiling water

Nutritional Facts Per Serving:

- Calories: 259.2
- Fat: 24.7g
- Carb: 6.3g
- Protein: 7g

Method:

1. Preheat the oven to 400F. Line baking sheet with parchment paper.

2. Beat the butter with garlic powder and set aside to use it for brushing.

3. Combine the salt, psyllium husk powder, baking powder, and almond flour. Add the butter along with the egg and mix until well combined.

4. Pour in the boiling water and mix until dough forms.

5. Divide the dough into 8 equal pieces and roll them into breadsticks.

6. Place in the baking sheet and bake for 15 minutes.

7. Brush the breadsticks with the garlic butter and bake for 5 minutes more.

8. Serve.

Savory Italian Crackers

Prep time: 10 minutes
Cook time: 15 minutes
Servings: 30

Ingredients:

- 1 ½ cup almond flour
- ¼ tsp. garlic powder
- ½ tsp. onion powder
- ½ tsp. thyme
- ¼ tsp. basil
- ¼ tsp. oregano
- ¾ tsp. salt
- 1 egg
- 2 Tbsp. olive oil

Nutritional Facts Per Serving:

- Calories: 63.5
- Fat: 5.8g
- Carb: 1.8g
- Protein: 2.1g

Method:

1. Preheat the oven to 350F. Line a baking sheet with parchment paper and set aside.
2. Combine all the ingredients in a food processor until dough forms.
3. Form the dough into a log and slice into thin crackers. Arrange the crackers onto the prepared baking sheet and bake for 10 to 15 minutes.
4. Cool and serve.

Easy Sesame Breadsticks

Prep time: 10 minutes
Cook time: 20 minutes
Servings: 5

Ingredients:

- 1 egg white
- 2 Tbsp. almond flour
- 1 tsp. Himalayan pink salt
- 1 Tbsp. extra virgin olive oil
- ½ tsp. sesame seeds

Nutritional Facts Per Serving:

- Calories: 53.6
- Fat: 5g
- Carb: 1.1g
- Protein: 1.6g

Method:

1. Preheat the oven to 320F. Line a baking sheet with parchment paper and set aside.
2. Whisk the egg white and add the flour as well as half each the salt and olive oil.
3. Knead until you get a smooth dough, divide into 5 pieces and roll into breadsticks.
4. Place on the prepared sheet, brush with the remaining olive oil, and sprinkle with the sesame seeds and remaining salt.
5. Bake for 20 minutes.

Keto Breadsticks

Prep time: 10 minutes
Cook time: 10 minutes
Servings: 8

Ingredients:

- 1/3 cup coconut flour
- 1/3 cup arrowroot flour
- ½ tsp. baking soda
- 1 ½ tsp. lemon juice
- 1 tsp. dried rosemary
- 3 Tbsp. water
- 1 egg
- 4 Tbsp. extra virgin olive oil, divided
- 1/8 tsp. garlic powder for topping
- 1/8 tsp. sea salt for topping

Nutritional Facts Per Serving:

- Calories: 216
- Fat: 15.8g
- Carb: 8.1g
- Protein: 3.1g

Method:

1. Preheat the oven to 350F.
2. Line a baking sheet with parchment paper and set aside.
3. Add all the ingredients to the food processor and pulse until well combined and the dough is formed.
4. Divide the dough into 8 equal balls and roll them into breadsticks.
5. Arrange on the prepared sheet, brush with olive oil, and sprinkle with garlic powder and salt.
6. Bake for 10 minutes.

Ultimate Keto Breadsticks

Prep time: minutes
Cook time: minutes
Servings: 20

Ingredients:

- ¼ cup coconut flour
- ¾ cup ground flax seeds
- 1 Tbsp. psyllium husk powder
- 1 cup almond flour
- 2 Tbsp. ground chia seeds
- 1 tsp. salt
- 1 cup lukewarm water, plus more if needed

Ingredients for the topping:

- 2 egg yolks, for brushing
- 4 Tbsp. mixed seeds
- 1 tsp. coarse sea salt

Nutritional Facts Per Serving:

- Calories: 75.2
- Fat: 9.6g
- Carb: 4.1g
- Protein: 3.5g

Method:

1. Combine the almond flour, psyllium husks, flax seeds, and coconut flour. Add the chia seeds, salt, and the water. Mix until dough is formed. Refrigerate for 20 minutes.

2. Preheat the oven to 350F. Line a baking sheet with parchment paper.

3. Divide the dough into 20 equal pieces and roll them with your hands forming breadsticks.

4. Arrange the breadsticks on the baking sheet and brush them with the egg yolks.

5. Sprinkle with seeds and salt and bake for 20 minutes.

6. Serve.

CONCLUSION

When you are ready to enjoy fresh bread and get your hands flurry, this keto bread cookbook serves up the perfect recipes to satisfy your bread cravings without the guilt or failing your diet. This book includes tried and tested keto bread and other baked goods recipes to help promote weight loss, increase energy, and suppress your hunger. Here you will find delicious ketogenic recipes which allow you to once again enjoy eating bread without all the carbohydrates.

Made in the USA
Coppell, TX
11 October 2021